Especially For

....

From

....

Date

....

3-MINUTE
DEVOTIONS
for Boys

90 Exciting Readings for
Men Under Construction

BARBOUR BOOKS
An Imprint of Barbour Publishing, Inc.

© 2015 by Barbour Publishing

Print ISBN 978-1-63058-678-2

eBook Editions:
Adobe Digital Edition (.epub) 978-1-63409-138-1
Kindle and MobiPocket Edition (.prc) 978-1-63409-139-8

Published by Barbour Books, an imprint of Barbour Publishing, Inc., 1810 Barbour Drive, Uhrichsville, Ohio 44683, www.barbourbooks.com

Our mission is to inspire the world with the life-changing message of the Bible.

Member of the
Evangelical Christian
Publishers Association

Printed in the United States of America.
06736 1019 SP

Introduction

Y ou have so much going on—school, friends, sports, and family activities. There's not always time to sit and read. That's what makes this devotional a great idea! These little three-minute readings will give you all the wisdom you need before heading out to school or to play. And you'll be learning a lot about yourself and God in a short time! Here's what each power-packed devotion looks like:

Minute 1: Reflect on God's Word.
Minute 2: Read real-life application and
   encouragement to build you into a man of God.
Minute 3: Pray.

Of course, these devotions aren't supposed to take the place of regular Bible reading. They're just a fun jump start to help you form a habit of spending time with God every day.

*Your word is a lamp to guide my feet
and a light for my path.*
PSALM 119:105 NLT

Let us move beyond the elementary teachings about Christ and be taken forward to maturity.

HEBREWS 6:1 NIV

No-Doubt-about-It Truth

Jesus answered, "I am the way and the truth and the life. No one comes to the Father except through me."

JOHN 14:6 NIV

The sun came up this morning. Food gives our bodies nourishment. Flowers don't grow in buckets of paint.

If these seem like things everyone should know, you're right. These are all true statements, but some people think each person can make a choice as to what he or she thinks is true. You might not think it makes sense to believe the sun never comes up, but we are told if someone really believes it, it's true for them even if we're standing in the sunshine looking for shade.

This idea is often used to say that God isn't real, Jesus was just a good man, and there's no heaven.

Jesus said He is the only way to God, He offers real life, and absolute truth comes from Him.

When people say they don't believe God it never really changes the *truth* that God's in control, loves people, and wants to rescue each of us from sinful choices.

God's Word is filled with truth. Read it. Believe it. Live it.

Dear God, You want me to believe You are truth. It would be hard to accept You if I never knew if You were lying. Your words are truth and can be trusted every minute of every day. Help me always believe that You're the Creator of no-doubt-about-it truth. Amen.

A Plan for Victory

For every child of God defeats this evil world, and we achieve this victory through our faith.

1 JOHN 5:4 NLT

What are you good at? Skateboarding, gaming, Ping-Pong?

We all have skills. Sometimes we win a trophy, plaque, or ribbon for being the best at what we do. The trophies get displayed, pictures taken, and memories made.

A lot of hard work goes into achieving anything really special. Sometimes this means we get up early, practice more, and work up a sweat.

God wants us to achieve one thing more than others. He may want us to get up early, practice hard, and use some energy.

When you play basketball you can't win a game

by sitting on the bench. When you're in a scholar's bowl you'll fail if you never study. When you live for God, you can't grow by refusing to follow the rules.

There are those around us who don't want us to succeed. They want us to make poor choices. They want us to lose interest in what God wants.

The only way we can win is to believe that God's plan for our lives can be trusted, that His truth should be followed, and that we're most like Him when we obey.

God, You want me to win. My greatest achievement is allowing You to help me defeat the evil plans my enemy has for me. Thanks for offering a plan for victory. Amen.

Don't Bring Me Down!

*The righteous choose their friends carefully,
but the way of the wicked leads them astray.*
PROVERBS **12:26** NIV

Imagine standing on a chair while a friend stands
in front of you on the floor. When someone says
"Go," you attempt to pull your friend up onto the
chair, while your friend tries just as hard to pull you
down to the floor. Who do you think will win?

Have you ever noticed how our personalities can
change when we are around certain people? How you
act around your family is probably different from how
you act around your friends. We all want to fit in, to
be like our friends. And our first response is to mimic
our friends' actions, whether good or bad. When a
friend makes bad choices, we're tugged toward bad
choices, too. The Bible tells us to choose our friends

wisely, because bad friends can cause us to do things we know are wrong. Just like the chair exercise, it's easier for a bad friend to pull us down and get us to follow him than it is to pull someone up and go after the good.

If you find yourself being pulled down, hang in there! Ask God for help, and He will draw you close to Himself.

Lord Jesus, please send good friends my way. Help me be a good friend who lifts up those around me, not a bad friend who brings others down. Thank You for being my good Friend. Amen.

Who We Hang Out With

*I am a friend to anyone who fears you—
anyone who obeys your commandments.*
PSALM 119:63 NLT

Friends are pretty wonderful. They listen to you, enjoy the same stuff, and are fun to hang out with.

God has always wanted us to be friendly to everyone. He invented love, so it just makes sense that we care about other people, but that doesn't mean all friends are created equal.

Some people want us to do things we know make God sad. Some think it's okay for you to follow God, but they don't want to. Other friends want to know God, too.

We should hang out the most with others who love God. We want to be around those friends who want to grow closer to God and want us to grow with them.

God's Word says we should find friends who build us up in our faith. Our best friends should be the ones who encourage us to follow God, and when we *do* make mistakes, these friends will help us to make things right as soon as possible.

Maybe you could be that kind of friend for someone today.

Heavenly Father, You want me to wisely choose my closest friends. It's important to You that I find friends who love You most of all. Help me be that kind of friend for someone else. If I'm not there yet, help me get there. Amen.

You're a Tour Guide

You are a chosen people. . . . God's very own possession. As a result, you can show others the goodness of God, for he called you out of the darkness into his wonderful light.

1 PETER 2:9 NLT

You're a spiritual tour guide. If that sounds strange think about your last visit to a museum. You saw lots of cool stuff, but without someone to tell you about each exhibit, you had to guess. Maybe you walked past displays because you had no idea why they were important.

When you're one of God's children you have the job of showing people what living for Jesus is all about. When you don't speak up others can't figure out why walking with Jesus is important.

If you've toured a cave, then you know what

it's like when they turn out the lights. All you can think of is how horrible it would be to always live in the darkness. That's what it's like for others who need to know what a life with Jesus is like. It's like discovering light in a dark cave. You get to show people the source of light. You get to point people to real hope. You get to share a message that changes lives. The best part is—you *get* to.

Dear God, You want me to take my job seriously. Help me show others why living for You is the only way to really discover life, light, and love. Amen.

Opportunities for All

"Give, and it will be given to you.
A good measure, pressed down, shaken together
and running over, will be poured into your lap.
For with the measure you use,
it will be measured to you."

LUKE 6:38 NIV

Jeff works with kids at church. In the drive-thru he paid for the meals of the two cars behind him just to show kindness. The kids in the church van had plenty to talk about when they saw what Jeff had done.

George is an average guy who works in the oil fields of Texas. He went out to eat and told the waiter he wanted to pay for the meal of a couple he'd never met at a different table. The waiter accidentally paid the wrong meal ticket, but George said it was all right and then said he still needed to pay for the original couple's meal. The waiter was inspired. George was overwhelmed because God allowed him to bless two families.

Just like Jeff and George, you could discover how much you enjoy giving the gift of kindness. Each random act of kindness blesses someone else, but it also does something amazing inside the heart of the giver.

Father, You want me to be kind to others. Help me recognize the many ways I can give. I am learning the skill from You. Thanks. Amen.

Ultimate Forgiveness

*If you, LORD, kept a record of sins, Lord,
who could stand? But with you there is forgiveness,
so that we can, with reverence, serve you.*
PSALM 130:3–4 NIV

eeping score. Holding a grudge. Do you know someone who keeps track of wrongs done to him? Every time someone hurts him, bad-mouths him, double-crosses him, it gets tallied up in his mind and held close to his heart. Maybe you find it hard to let go of offenses against you.

Can you imagine if God kept a record of wrongs done to Him? Sins are wrongs that we commit against God. The truth is, there wouldn't be enough books in the world to hold the number of wrongs against God. But there's good news! Through salvation, we have ultimate forgiveness in Christ.

Forgiveness is the key to tearing up that book of wrongs that we hold so closely in our lives, too. If God can forgive *all* the sins committed against Him, we can forgive the ones committed against us. It's not always easy. Some wrongs may take a lifetime to forgive. But we can ask God, the example of forgiveness, to help us forgive.

Thank You, Lord, for not keeping a record of wrongs! Please forgive me for hanging on to my own list of wrongs. Help me to let go and forgive those who have hurt me. I give You my pain and anger; please give me Your love and peace instead. Amen.

What's Left to Worry About?

"This is my command—be strong and courageous! Do not be afraid or discouraged. For the Lord your God is with you wherever you go."

JOSHUA 1:9 NLT

Sometimes the latest news can be frightening. Lots of bad things can happen. It has always been that way, at least since the first sin by Adam and Eve. People make bad choices. Those decisions cause hurt, anger, and disappointment. For many people those choices cause fear.

We should always be smart. This might mean that we stay away from things we know could be harmful, but the fear we feel is a waste of emotion and will never change the outcome.

Our fears could be about something we don't understand, about a location, or about a person. God never wants us to be afraid. If we really believe He is in control, then what's left to worry about?

God is always with us. God's got this.

Be strong. Be courageous. Be brave. Be bold. Be fearless. Be assured that the God who created you is able to care for you better than anyone who has ever lived.

Lord, You want me to know worry is my enemy. When I do find myself fearful help me remember that because You have promised to take care of things I can relax. Worry never makes me feel good, so help me stop making fear a habit. Make me strong and courageous. Help me be brave. Amen.

Never Alone

"Don't be afraid, for I am with you. Don't be discouraged, for I am your God. I will strengthen you and help you. I will hold you up with my victorious right hand."

ISAIAH **41:10** NLT

If a child can't find his mom in a store he wants to be found—quickly. The game of hide-and-seek isn't much fun if nobody looks for you. Thinking you're alone can make you feel desperate, fearful, and sad.

Even adults hate loneliness. We all look for friendships that show someone cares about us.

David was chased away from Israel by King Saul and spent years away from those he cared about. Jesus was all alone when He was tempted. Yet God used David to write psalms that comfort us, and Jesus showed us that being alone allows us to trust God more.

The natural reaction to being alone is fear and discouragement. God's answer is to strengthen us and help us defeat anxiety and frustration.

Many discover a way to be alone without feeling lonely. How? Remembering God is always with us.

Talk to Him. He's a great listener.

Dear God, You're all I need. When I'm alone You want me to remember I'm never really alone. You give me the strength I need and You hold on to me when I think everything is breaking apart. Thanks for reminding me that I don't have to be discouraged. Help me refuse to be afraid. Amen.

Your Pet Sin

*"If you do what is right, will you not be accepted?
But if you do not do what is right, sin is crouching
at your door; it desires to have you, but
you must rule over it."*

GENESIS 4:7 NIV

Everybody has one: a pet sin. You know, it's the sin
you hang on to. You keep coming back to it like a
favorite T-shirt. When life gets tough or things don't
go as planned, it bubbles up from deep within and
rears its ugly head. For some, it's pride, envy, worry,
fear, rebellion, self-centeredness, disobedience,
anger. . .you fill in the blank.

The Bible says "sin is crouching at your door; it
desires to have you, but you must rule over it." Sin is
always there, like a lion waiting to pounce. It wants
to eat you alive. But with God's help, we are stronger

than our sin, not the other way around.

If you are struggling with sin today, seek God in prayer. And ask for help from family and leaders in your church. You have the power to stand up against sin. . .and win!

Lord Jesus, You know what my pet sin is. Help me to turn to You instead. I don't want to make excuses for my sin. Be in control of my life so that I can rule over my sin. Prompt me to ask forgiveness when I need to. Amen.

Everything Under Control

*Human anger does not produce the
righteousness God desires.*

JAMES 1:20 NLT

Our anger proves that we think laws should be
followed. We become angry when we believe
someone isn't playing by the rules. Anger gives
people a glimpse into our hearts.

There is another side to anger. You can become
angry when someone discovers *you* haven't been
playing by the rules. You may believe they have
no right to point out your faults. You treat the
conversation like a sport, and you're on defense,
ready to attack.

God says that neither type of anger leads to a
good place. Why? God wants us to love others, but
anger tends to hate. God wants us to forgive, but

anger wants justice. God wants us to be peaceful, but anger rips peace away like Velcro.

We're supposed to live differently, but anger invites us to hold tightly to responses that God says are off-limits.

Anger isn't a sin, but what we do when we become angry can cause us to sin. Let God help you change your responses, and anger won't show up as much.

Dear God, You want me to love, forgive, and live peacefully with others, but I can't do that if I let anger control the way I respond. Help me remember You have everything under control, You know what everyone does, and You care about my response. Help me learn to act more like You, especially when I'm angry. Amen.

Work Is God's Idea

*A lazy person's way is blocked with briers,
but the path of the upright is an open highway.*
PROVERBS 15:19 NLT

ive more minutes, Mom!" "Do I have to clean my room *today*?" "I hate taking the trash out!"

Have you ever said any of these things? Maybe you said something similar today.

God wants us to spend time with Him every day, but He also knows that when we don't have something good to do, we can be tempted to do the wrong thing. Work is God's idea. It teaches responsibility, an attitude of service, and helps us discover purpose.

You don't have to have a job to work. You can serve others, your family, or work to learn new skills. Doing nothing makes it much easier to continue doing nothing.

When you can't see anything good in the work you accomplish, you can begin to think that nothing good exists. You might think that there is no purpose, no promise, and no possibility of enjoying life.

That's why God wants us to do everything for Him. If we work for Him then *everything* we do is meaningful.

God, You want me to enjoy work. That's hard for me to understand because cleaning my room is not fun. Help me learn the importance of work. Help me see that You have created me for a purpose, and I can't do what You want me to do if I don't do anything. Amen.

Reasons to Appreciate Others

*"A new command I give you: Love one another.
As I have loved you, so you must love one
another. By this everyone will know that you
are my disciples, if you love one another."*
JOHN 13:34–35 NIV

Jesus wants us to love people. This includes those who take care of us, our friends, and those we've just met.

We show love by appreciating the good things others do for us. This can seem hard because it means we'll have to think about and name the good things that others do—out loud. It's easier with a parent who sacrifices to help us, but harder with a brother or sister who gets on our nerves. It might be easy with a pastor who is kind and helpful, but harder with a friend or neighbor whose great skill seems to be annoying people.

When you show appreciation you're saying that the person you're talking to plays an important role in your life. They have value even when they are a little frustrating. That can be hard to admit, but it shows love and can be a way for God to improve your friendships.

Jesus, You want me to follow You. Help me show love to others by deciding to show appreciation to the lady who serves lunch at school, to my family, teachers, friends, neighbors, and even the guy who isn't always nice. Help me find reasons to appreciate others, and then let them know. Amen.

The Work in Homework

Work hard and become a leader;
be lazy and become a slave.
PROVERBS 12:24 NLT

ave you ever felt like you're spinning your
wheels when it comes to homework? Maybe the
work is too hard and you can't figure out what you are
supposed to do, so you just give up. Maybe you have
a hard time staying focused. So the work just piles up,
and you feel like you're drowning. Maybe the work
is too easy, and you don't see the point in doing the
busy work the teacher gives you.

Doing the work assigned to you, diligently, with
care, wanting to do what is right, is important if
you want to be placed in a position of leadership.
If the work is too hard, talk to your teacher or seek
out a tutor at your school. If you are having trouble

focusing, ask for tips from teachers or your parents. They will be able to point you in the right direction. If the work is too easy, do it anyway. The only way your teachers will know you need to be challenged more is if they see your completed work.

Lord, help me to be diligent with my homework. When I am struggling, show me the right person to go to for help. Give me the determination and willpower to be consistent in my work. Amen.

An Honorable Demonstration

"Do to others whatever you would like them to do to you. This is the essence of all that is taught in the law and the prophets."
MATTHEW 7:12 NLT

It's hard to believe that someone respects you when they do things they know you don't like. Respect means valuing other people by considering their needs as important as your own.

When the Bible gives us the "Golden Rule" we're reminded of something important to God. We show respect by honoring the interests, needs, and concerns of people who'll be happy to know you value them enough to be kind.

When we show respect to others we often begin to receive respect in return. Showing honor to others doesn't mean you repay respect only when they're respectful. Sometimes you'll need to be the first to show honor. It doesn't even mean that you have to agree with their choices. It just means that you help them see that God can change the way Christians respond.

God treats us the way He wants to be treated, too. He loved, showed faithfulness, and invited friendship first. It's easier to respect others when we respect God first.

Dear God, You want me to show honor to other people. They could be older or younger, stronger or weaker, easy to love or hard to like. Help me remember You have always been interested in me. I should be interested in others. Amen.

Are You Ready to Help?

*"Come, follow me," Jesus said, "and I will send
you out to fish for people." At once they
left their nets and followed him.*
MARK 1:17–18 NIV

When your family needs someone to repair the car or roof they call a professional.

However, God looks to the most unexpected people and says, "Are you ready to help?"

You may not feel like you have the skills to help God, but God gives us *everything* we need to get the job done.

When Jesus spoke to the men who would become His disciples He said, "Come follow Me." He didn't ask if they had special skills or work experience. Jesus wanted the disciples to know they couldn't do the work on their own, but they would never have to.

When someone you admire is ready to tackle a project and they look at you and say, "Are you ready to help?" it's a huge moment for you. Even if you have no idea what you're doing you will learn from someone who has more wisdom and is willing to teach—just the way Jesus taught His disciples. Learn from Jesus; become His disciple.

God, You want me to be ready to say yes when You call. I don't have to know it all to understand that You can still use me. That's pretty incredible. Thanks for inviting me to help. I look forward to learning from You. Amen.

I Can Change the World?

Neither in the days of the judges who led Israel nor in the days of the kings of Israel and the kings of Judah had any such Passover been observed. But in the eighteenth year of King Josiah, this Passover was celebrated to the LORD in Jerusalem.

2 KINGS 23:22–23 NIV

The Bible tells us of a young king named Josiah. He became king when he was eight years old. Imagine having the weight of a whole kingdom on your shoulders at that age! Before Josiah became king, there were a lot of bad kings that caused Judah (the southern kingdom of Israel) to worship gods other than their God. These other gods required their followers to sell themselves and even sacrifice their children by throwing them in a fire in order to have success in life. Single-handedly, Josiah turned the country away from worshipping false gods and toward following the God who brought them out of Egypt hundreds of years before.

Sometimes others start to follow false gods because it looks fun or different. Following Jesus can feel restrictive. Pretty soon, though, the idols they are chasing after leave them feeling empty, and they may not see any way out of the situation they are in. They need a friend to come alongside them and tell them that Jesus is waiting. You can turn the whole world upside down for someone that way. You can change the whole world for one person by pointing them to Jesus.

Jesus, I want to be a world changer! Lead me to the person who needs me most. Give me the courage to point them to You. Help me to get rid of my own idols—those things I choose instead of You—so that others will see Your love in me. Amen.

When You Don't Feel Like It

[Jesus said], "If you love me,
keep my commands."
JOHN 14:15 NIV

You don't have to plan on sinning to do the
wrong thing. Sin is easy to find, looks like a lot
of fun, and never reminds you of the consequences.

Sin is an easier choice than obedience. Maybe
that's because our feelings love sin. People excuse
their sin by saying it felt right or that they were
having so much fun they couldn't help themselves.

Avoiding sin is a decision you should make
before you get into a situation where it *feels* like you
have no choice but to sin. If you know God doesn't
want you to lie, then you need to decide that truth is
what will come out of your mouth.

Jesus said that keeping His commandments

(obedience) is the best way to show that we love Him. He didn't say, "If you love Me, apologize daily."

We'll get it wrong. We'll sin. We'll wonder why we didn't obey. This is why God made sure we'd always be forgiven through Jesus' death on the cross.

Instead of seeking God's forgiveness as our regular reaction we should avoid sin by obeying God—even when we don't *feel* like it.

Dear God, You want me to obey. When I accepted Jesus and His forgiveness I started my friendship with You, and I trust You most when I obey Your commands. Help me always decide Your way is the best way. Amen.

Stand Guard

*Timothy, guard what God has entrusted to you.
Avoid godless, foolish discussions with those who
oppose you with their so-called knowledge.*

1 TIMOTHY 6:20 NLT

imothy was just a few years older than you. The
apostle Paul had been training Timothy in what
it looks like to be a Christian. Not just someone that
says God is cool, but one who really knew what God
wanted him to do.

Timothy had gone through basic training. He
knew the truth. He had a great teacher. He was
following God. Yet there was one more thing Paul
asked Timothy to do—stand guard.

What did he have to guard against? Someone
stronger? Timothy was to guard against foolish
discussions with those who didn't really believe in God.

We also need to stand guard. It becomes easier to change the way you think when others chip away at the truth you've been learning. You may not see the danger at first. After all, they're just words. If you don't stand guard, then words that question God can change the way you think, act, and believe.

Stick with the basics you find in the Bible. The truth found there is the best way to defend, or guard, everything you're learning.

Lord, Your words help me know how to really live. Help me avoid those who don't respect You. Help me grow in my faith. Help me share what I know. Help me pray for those who need to understand. Amen.

No Acting Required

The fruit of the Spirit is love, joy, peace,
forbearance, kindness, goodness, faithfulness,
gentleness and self-control.
GALATIANS 5:22–23 NIV

Sometimes being on our best behavior is like acting on stage. We say and do one thing, but it's not really who we are or what we believe. That's why just trying to behave never works very long. It's much easier to be yourself than to act like someone different.

Telling the truth, being kind to friends, and showing kindness are things your family would be proud to see in you. If you think you might be acting when you behave this way, be patient. God may have big plans for you.

The fruit of the Spirit is proof that God is working

in your life. When you obey what God asks, you will be more loving, joyful, peaceful, patient, kind, good, faithful, gentle, and self-controlled. No acting required.

God wants you to do the right thing, but by growing as a Christian those "right things" become much easier because when you obey God you get closer to the plans He's always had for you.

Dear God, You want me to show signs of growth. You want me to see value in obeying You. Sometimes it seems like I'm pulling up the roots of love, kindness, or self-control that You've planted in my life. Help me to be patient enough to see Your fruit grow so I can be the young man You want me to be. Amen.

Sons of God

See what great love the Father has lavished on us, that we should be called children of God! And that is what we are!

1 JOHN 3:1 NIV

A family adopted an infant, but soon after discovering that they had been chosen by the birth mom for the adoption, the couple found out that they were going to have a baby! They excitedly welcomed the "twins" into their lives. Even though the babies have two different biological sets of parents, they belong to the same family. They have the same mom and dad, the same brothers and sisters. They are seen through the eyes of love.

God wants to adopt us into His family. That's the reason Jesus died for our sins. That was the price for our adoption. He wants us to be a part of His family so much that He sent His own Son, Jesus, to pay the steep price with His life. . .just so we can "be called children of God!" We may come from different birth families, but we are God's children, seen through the loving eyes of our heavenly Father.

Thank You, God, for loving me! I know there are times when I am unlovable, but You still want me to be part of Your family. Thank You for adopting me through Your Son's life. I love You, Father. Amen.

Temptation's Answer

Jesus answered, "It is written: 'Man shall not live on bread alone, but on every word that comes from the mouth of God.'"

MATTHEW 4:4 NIV

When Jesus spent time on our planet He was tempted by the devil. Jesus hadn't eaten in over a month and was tired and hungry. It would have been easy for Jesus to create His favorite foods, but when the devil tried to get Jesus to turn stones into bread He said, *"Man shall not live on bread alone, but on every word that comes from the mouth of God."*

In that moment Jesus taught everyone that the Bible was not only useful in learning more about God, but that it's what we should use when we're tempted to do something we know is wrong.

The Bible is important, but if we don't know what

the Bible says, we *will* make wrong decisions.

When we're tempted to say something mean about someone we might remind ourselves that we are supposed *"to speak evil of no one, to avoid quarreling, to be gentle, and to show perfect courtesy toward all people"* (Titus 3:2 ESV).

Knowing the Bible can help us remember who we are, what we do, and how we should live.

Lord, You want me to really know what You've said. You left me with Your words in the Bible. I should never be confused if I look for Your thoughts in Your Word. Help me read it often. Amen.

Setting His Example

Be on guard. Stand firm in the faith.
Be courageous. Be strong.
And do everything with love.

1 Corinthians 16:13–14 nlt

When you don't love someone it's difficult to stand up for them when they're in trouble. When you don't love God, it's easy to be afraid. When you have no love for other people you can't stand strong because you never see anything worth fighting for.

God created us to be guardians, ambassadors, soldiers, and guys who care about other people.

He wants us to set His example for others to see. We never need to apologize for doing the right thing. We stand up for His truth and for those who need encouragement. He's given us a big job with big responsibilities, opportunities, and just the right amount of adventure.

We stand for something more important than sports and hobbies. We are strong in sharing a message that changes lives. We are courageous because everyone needs to know Jesus. We love because He loved us first.

The message we share can change lives. Refusing to speak up when someone really needs to hear what we have to say doesn't help them see the love we're supposed to share. Be courageous. Speak up.

Dear God, You want me to show that Your message is worth sharing. I can't do that if I seem to apologize for knowing You. Help me be courageous because Your message is something everyone should hear. Amen.

24

Turn the Other Cheek

Since God loved us that much, we surely ought to love each other. No one has ever seen God. But if we love each other, God lives in us, and his love is brought to full expression in us.

1 JOHN 4:11–12 NLT

Nick was in middle school when other kids started picking on him. He was called names and laughed at. One girl was particularly cruel. She enjoyed targeting his appearance and tearing him down. It became a daily ritual. Nick did everything he could to avoid the girl, but she sought him out. Nick's mom spoke with the teachers, but that didn't seem to help. Every week, Nick would ask the guys in his small group for prayer. He would get all kinds of advice on how to get back at the girl, but Nick knew he was a Christian. . .and needed to act like one.

Loving others isn't easy, especially when they hurt us. But if we are going to love the way God loves us, we need to love even when it is hard.

Think about this: we may be someone's first experience with God's love. Being kind and loving toward others, even our "enemies," could lead someone to Jesus.

In our own strength, we can't love the unlovable. But God gives us His Spirit to help us through the tough times.

Thank You, God, for loving me—a sinner. Help me to see others as You see them, and give me strength to stand strong in love, even when loving others is difficult. Amen.

25

Within the Fence

Follow God's example, therefore, as dearly loved children and walk in the way of love, just as Christ loved us and gave himself up for us as a fragrant offering and sacrifice to God.

EPHESIANS 5:1–2 NIV

hen the Bible tells us to "follow God's example" it means He leads and models how we should live. When He says we're "dearly loved children" we know He accepts us. When we "walk in love" we choose to follow God's greatest commandment. When we see what Jesus did to show His love for us we understand how important love is to God.

God created everything with a purpose. That includes you. When you "walk in love" you're living within the boundary of His commands. Like a spiritual fence, God's commands give plenty of freedom as long as you stay within the border.

When a dog leaves the protection of a fenced yard it can get into trouble, get hurt, or lost. There are many more good things inside the fence than outside.

Spiritual fences aren't designed to make you miss what you shouldn't do, but to give you the space to do something special using the safety of God's protection—within the fence.

Father, You want me to walk with You. Everything with a purpose has directions that must be followed. When I try to do things on my own I discover why directions are important. Help me find joy in following You. Amen.

26

Show an Interest

Don't look out only for your own interests, but take an interest in others, too.
PHILIPPIANS 2:4 NLT

When your favorite store hires workers they want people who really care for the needs of their customers. When you're sick you want a doctor or nurse to help. When you order at a restaurant you never expect to hear a waiter say, "Get it yourself."

The things that make someone a valuable employee are the things that help you show others the love Jesus gave to you. Show an interest in others, be ready to help them, listen to what they have to say, treat them with respect, and don't be rude.

When we're more interested in what we want, talk more than we listen, and have no interest in helping others we don't show respect. We also don't give others a reason to believe that God makes a difference.

We should enjoy our hobbies, but the things we're interested in should never become so important we don't feel we can make time for others. You can't develop friendships if you don't share time and attention with others.

Dear God, You want me to care for others. I can't do that if all I can think about is me. Sometimes the only way other people can see the good things You can do is when someone like me shows them good things You have taught. Keep teaching me so I can keep showing them. Amen.

27

What's That Irritating Sound?

Do all things without grumbling or disputing, that you may be blameless and innocent, children of God without blemish in the midst of a crooked and twisted generation, among whom you shine as lights in the world, holding fast to the word of life.
PHILIPPIANS 2:14–16 ESV

It's easy to grumble when you're asked to do something you don't want to do. You want a rewards program that lets you get by without doing a chore, or maybe there's someone else in the family who could do it this time.

Requests for help come at the worst times. You have a friend over, you're playing a game, or you're tired. You wish the whole *chore* thing could be planned without your participation.

Sometimes whining sounds like a foreign

language to your family. They may not understand what you're saying, but they know it's irritating.

God's Word says something like "Quit complaining, whining, and whimpering. That's what people who don't know God do. You're supposed to help people see Jesus, not irritate them with the sound of your pity parties."

When you think about what God does for you, any complaining seems disrespectful. Try thanking God. It changes the sound of complaints to words of praise.

Heavenly Father, You want my words to help others, not make them cringe. I want to help people see You, not make people wish they had earplugs. Help me speak words that overlook things I would normally complain about. Amen.

28

Power of God

*Where is the man who thinks he knows a lot?
Where is the man who thinks he has all the
answers? God has made the wisdom of this
world look foolish. In His wisdom, He did not
allow man to come to know Him through the
wisdom of this world. It pleased God to save
men from the punishment of their sins
through preaching the Good News.*

1 CORINTHIANS 1:20–21 NLV

Every couple of months, a local youth group
serves lunch at a soup kitchen. As they help
hand out the food, they see a side of life they wouldn't
normally see. Men, women, and even kids come to the
shelter for a meal. They have so little. . .when the kids
from the youth group have so much.

Why do some people live better than others?

Why can't God, with all His power, come in and change things. . .make things fair? The Bible says that the Jews demanded signs. They wanted God to show His power in a big way. They wanted Him to blow their minds, do something flashy.

Isn't that what we want? For God to do something flashy and take care of whatever problem we see in our lives or in other people's lives? While we may not understand God's ways, He is always at work. His wisdom is much greater than any solution our minds can create.

Lord, thank You for working Your power in my heart. Help me be careful in what I ask of You. Open my eyes to Your power at work around me. Amen.

29

Nothing Left to Learn?

There is more hope for fools than for people who think they are wise.

PROVERBS 26:12 NLT

When you're filled with pride you believe everyone already knows how cool you are, but if they don't then you're ready to pass out posters listing all the reasons why you're better than just about anyone in your zip code. You walk and talk a certain way, and then try to make people think they should be honored you decided to notice them.

This may seem like a good way to prove you're awesome, but to most other people they don't see the same thing. They're paying a lot of attention to your actions, which seem to say, "You will never be as important as me."

Instead of people liking you more they end up

not wanting to be around you. Pride gets about the same reaction as someone showing up to a fancy restaurant in a clown suit. You get noticed, but not in a good way.

God's Word says there is more hope for a fool than for someone full of pride. Maybe that's because the fool can learn while the prideful person never believes they have anything left to learn.

Dear God, You want me to remember pride doesn't look good on me. I need to remember pride points to me and never makes room for others. Help me honor You and others by spending less time listing the things I've done. Amen.

30

Wrong Choices

I acknowledged my sin to you and did not cover up my iniquity. I said, "I will confess my transgressions to the Lᴏʀᴅ." And you forgave the guilt of my sin.

Pꜱᴀʟᴍ 32:5 NIV

Tucker really wanted a pack of gum. His mom said no. Waiting in line to check out he kept looking at the gum. When he couldn't stand it anymore he grabbed a pack and stuck it in his pocket.

The Bible calls this stealing. A security guard stopped Tucker before he left the store and said, "Do you have something that doesn't belong to you?"

Tucker's face grew hot, and he denied having taken anything, but the security guard watched him take the gum and knew the exact pocket where it was hidden.

When we confess our sin, what we're really doing

is admitting that we made wrong choices and we want to make things right.

God knows what we've done. We can't hide it from Him. When we try, we look like Tucker trying to convince everyone that he hadn't taken the gum.

Admit that you've sinned, don't try to cover it up, and let God forgive you. Then, go make things right.

Lord, You don't want me to believe a lie. You know every decision I make. You say that sin leads to death, but Jesus came to give life. Help me admit when I make wrong choices so I can always choose Jesus over sin. Amen.

31

Great Expectations

Jesus said to him, "Thomas, because you have seen Me, you believe. Those are happy who have never seen Me and yet believe!" Jesus did many other powerful works in front of His followers. They are not written in this book. But these are written so you may believe that Jesus is the Christ, the Son of God. When you put your trust in Him, you will have life that lasts forever through His name.
JOHN 20:29–31 NLV

We all have expectations. Sometimes what we expect doesn't match up with what really is. When that happens, we feel confused or frustrated or even let down.

When Jesus walked the earth, the Jews were looking for a Messiah. They were expecting a certain type of savior. . .one who would free them from their

Roman captivity. What they got was Jesus. He wasn't at all what they expected! He didn't come to start a military revolution. He came with a different agenda altogether.

Why is Jesus different? He is *the* Messiah and the Son of God. He came to give us life in His name. The book of John was written to give you evidence so that you would believe the truth about Jesus. He offers something greater than freedom from earthly troubles. He is the path to eternal life. He far exceeds our expectations!

Jesus, as I learn more about You, help me set aside those experiences that give me a wrong idea of You. Help me to see You as You are. Amen.

32

Live in Peace

What is causing the quarrels and fights among you? Don't they come from the evil desires at war within you? You want what you don't have, so you scheme and kill to get it. You are jealous of what others have, but you can't get it, so you fight and wage war to take it away from them.

JAMES 4:1–2 NLT

When we don't get along with others it's usually because we don't agree. The other person may not like your ideas or you may not like theirs. When people disagree they usually get angry. Some people will hurt others when they're angry. Some will hurt back. Some never forgive.

We don't have to agree with others to live in peace with them. When we hurt someone because they hurt us we can expect the hurt to continue.

If arguing isn't bad enough there are many sins that follow. You could wind up trying to steal something that doesn't belong to you, wanting something that can never be yours, and fighting can even lead to murder.

Standing up for what's right is a good thing. Fighting in order to have something that isn't yours is not.

Dear God, You remind me that quarrels aren't the best use of time. Help me be pleased when good things happen to other people. I know I would want them to be happy for me. Help me learn that fights rarely lead to happy endings. Amen.

33

The Seeds We Plant

Don't be misled—you cannot mock the justice of God. You will always harvest what you plant. Those who live only to satisfy their own sinful nature will harvest decay and death from that sinful nature. But those who live to please the Spirit will harvest everlasting life from the Spirit.

GALATIANS 6:7–8 NLT

Pick a vegetable you love to eat. Okay. Now imagine planting seeds so you can eventually eat fresh veggies. Wait! There's just one problem. Instead of using your favorite veggie seeds you decide that since you had a package of daisy seeds you'd plant those instead. You water the ground, make sure it has plenty of sunshine, and then wait for your one-of-a-kind veggie.

But only daisies grow in your garden.

It doesn't make any sense to plant the wrong thing hoping that the right vegetable will grow.

God wants us to know you can't plant anger seeds and expect a peace flower. You can't toss in seeds of bitterness and expect a crop of forgiveness. The hatred plant never produced love.

God is aware of what we plant in our lives. Unless the bad seed is removed your plants will produce a crop you don't want.

Father, You show me how to grow crops that help me,
but I'm always free to plant bad seeds if I want.
Help me sow the seeds you give so that love,
forgiveness, hope, joy, and patience can grow. Amen.

34

The Wise Remember

*Let the one who is wise heed these things and
ponder the loving deeds of the Lord.*
PSALM 107:43 NIV

Sometimes all we can think of is ourselves. We
remember the things someone did to us, the
homework we don't think we have time to do, and a
family member we think is rude. We think only about
our problems and accomplishments, but when it's all
about us there's no room for God.

God's Word says we're wise when we think about
the ways God shows us His love. We find it in the
way He created the sun to shine and the moon to
glow. He loves us in providing food to eat. His love is
found in the air we breathe, the things we enjoy, the
forgiveness He offers, and how He rescued us from
the punishment of sin.

Look hard enough and find God's love in the affection of a pet, the company of friends, and in people who make you smile.

God has blessed you. Spend time remembering what He has done for you and watch your attitude change from thinking about *you* to thinking about God and the *other* people He made.

Dear God, You want me to remember Your faithfulness. You're an amazing God, and the things You have made are incredible. Help me think about You first. I want to know what You want, and I can't do that when all I think about is me. Amen.

35

Reading God's Word

He left Babylon on the first day of the first month, and came to Jerusalem on the first day of the fifth month, because the good hand of his God was upon him. For Ezra had set his heart to learn the Law of the Lord, to live by it, and to teach His Laws in Israel.

EZRA 7:9–10 NLV

A father traveled a lot for work and had rules for his son when he was gone. One of his rules was that for every minute the boy watched TV, he had to read his Bible for that many minutes. So a thirty-minute TV show meant reading the Bible for thirty minutes, too. The boy got creative with his reading. He bought a pocket Bible and carried it wherever he went. He would read on the bus, before school started, and after he finished his homework. Pretty soon he had logged enough minutes of Bible reading to watch his favorite TV show.

The Bible tells us that Ezra devoted himself to the study of God's Word. He did more than pick up a devotional book or open a Bible now and then. It says he devoted himself. He was disciplined and regular in his study. And once he learned something, he obeyed it. The Bible tells us the result was that God's good hand was upon him. Wow!

God, I want to know what the Bible says. Let that desire drive me to study Your Word. Give me a mind of understanding and a heart of obedience. Amen.

36

A Bad Case of the Gimmies

Then he said to them, "Watch out! Be on your guard against all kinds of greed; life does not consist in an abundance of possessions."
LUKE 12:15 NIV

Your best friend has the latest gaming system. The popular guys at school have the hottest athletic shoes. You want them. You also want an iPod, popular movies, and trendy clothes.

It's easy to think that if we just had more *things* we'd be satisfied, but we're not.

The more we own, the more time we spend taking care of stuff. Greed steals your ability to really live. How? When all you can think about is having what you don't own you can't enjoy what you already have. You'll spend less time with family and friends. You'll own things that break. You'll learn that what's really awesome today isn't so much next week.

When greed overcomes you, you might demand that your family get something for you. When you have a really bad case of the *gimmies* you'll be tempted to hurt, lie, or cheat to get something. God's always had a better way to live life.

Dear God, You want me to see other people as more important than stuff. You sent Your Son to bring life, not new stuff. You want my treasure to be with You in the choices I make that show others that Your love is available even if we own nothing. Help me keep a safe distance from greed. Amen.

37

Invest Wisely

Don't copy the behavior and customs of this world, but let God transform you into a new person by changing the way you think. Then you will learn to know God's will for you, which is good and pleasing and perfect.

ROMANS 12:2 NLT

When you take money to the bank and put it in a savings account it will earn more money. This is called an investment. Wise people invest in decisions that lead to God-honoring futures.

God wants us to invest our time, money, and choices wisely. Since our future is with Him in heaven it doesn't make a lot of sense to try to look, act, and sound like everyone around us.

Spending a lot of time doing things that don't help us become more like Jesus teaches us to be more like people who don't know Him.

We should prepare to live in heaven. This means we change the way we think, we learn God's plans to make us more like Him, and we follow those plans.

When people can't tell a difference between us and someone who doesn't follow Jesus, then we might need to ask God for some help. He's always ready to lead when we're ready to follow.

Father, You want me to make every minute count. You want my life to look like that of someone who takes You seriously. Help me seek Your words so I know more about how You want me to invest my life. Amen.

38

The Holy Club

Work at living a holy life, for those who are not holy will not see the Lord. Look after each other so that none of you fails to receive the grace of God. Watch out that no poisonous root of bitterness grows up to trouble you, corrupting many.

HEBREWS 12:14–15 NLT

A group of guys at church started a Holy Club. They would hang out together, but they wouldn't let just anyone join. Anyone who had committed really big sins couldn't be part of the group and never could because of their sin.

Is that what holiness is? The religious leaders during Jesus' life seemed to think so. They placed so many rules on people that there was no way anyone could possibly follow them. These religious leaders were the original Holy Club, and they looked down on anyone who tried to get closer to Jesus.

The Bible says we should make every effort to be holy. That sounds like we should follow a bunch of rules to be good. But not if we look at what the word *holy* means. It actually means to be dedicated or connected to God. Our "goodness" has nothing to do with holiness. It's God's grace that deals with our sin, not our being good. But we can choose to be holy. We can choose to be dedicated to God and His purpose. Jesus welcomes sinners in His club.

Thank You, Jesus, for letting me be a part of Your Holy Club. I give my life for You to use for Your good purpose. Amen.

39

Kingdom Curiosity

"Seek the Kingdom of God above all else,
and live righteously, and he will
give you everything you need."
MATTHEW 6:33 NLT

Are you curious? Some people like to know how things work while others are curious about history, sports, or music.

We should be curious, but God wants us to be most curious about the future He has planned for us.

We can be curious about many things that will never lead us closer to God. These distractions may be a waste of time and delay our learning what God wants us to do.

God's Word never says, "Seek first gaming cheat codes," or "Seek first the football field," or even, "Seek first to get straight As." While there may be nothing

wrong with gaming, sports, or schoolwork, God tells us to "seek the Kingdom of God."

Many people know they should seek God, but never really do. A church service on the weekend is about as curious as they get. God wants us to be even more inquisitive. He gives us permission to be curious every day of the year.

Get curious.

Dear God, You never hide from me, but You always want me to seek You. Your Word shows me the best way to live, the reasons to love, and the gifts You have for me. If I'm not curious enough to read what You say I may never know that You have plans—for me. Help me seek. Help me find. Amen.

40

The Words We Speak

Don't use foul or abusive language.
Let everything you say be good and helpful,
so that your words will be an encouragement
to those who hear them.

EPHESIANS 4:29 NLT

Words are pretty important. But it's not just the words; it's also *how* we say them. You can speak the right words, but in a way that causes others to think you don't really mean them.

Sometimes you can use words that distract people from what you're really saying. This can be confusing to the person who hears you speak.

We may tell other people that we love God and want to follow Him, but then use what God calls *"foul or abusive language."* These may be words we hear other people say every day, but when we say them we make people think we aren't serious about following God. Why? These words don't show what God is like. God wants us to speak differently.

It's easy to be abusive in the way we talk or use language we know is inappropriate, but God says, *"Let everything you say be good and helpful, so that your words will be an encouragement to those who hear them."*

Heavenly Father, You want me to choose my words carefully. I should use words that encourage others, and I shouldn't abuse or offend people with my language. Help me to speak words that honor You and show and tell more about You. Amen.

41

Start Well—Finish Strong

[Daniel said], "Praise be to the name of God for ever and ever; wisdom and power are his.... He gives wisdom to the wise and knowledge to the discerning."
DANIEL 2:20–21 NIV

The Bible has stories of people who blew it. God rescued murderers, liars, cheaters, and all sorts of untrustworthy people. Maybe He wanted to share their stories so we would see that He really can change the way we think, act, and live.

We see so many people who may have started badly, but they end up finishing well. God loves to rescue people from sinful choices.

But God is also interested in helping us learn to make good choices and to make those a part of our everyday lives. We aren't perfect, but we can make following God a priority. God wants us to

start well and finish strong.

Daniel was one of those individuals. He trusted God, obeyed His laws, and served in difficult conditions.

If you've heard of Daniel you may remember that he was thrown in a pit filled with hungry lions as a punishment for praying. He trusted God and was kept safe.

Dear God, You want me to accept Your rescue plan no matter where I am. Daniel made decisions early in his life to follow You, and he continued to follow throughout his life. You can rescue me from bad choices, but You're also pleased when I trust—and obey—today. Thanks for rescuing me. Amen.

42

Competition

Anyone who competes as an athlete does not receive the victor's crown except by competing according to the rules.

2 TIMOTHY 2:5 NIV

thlete. Victor. Compete. Is the Bible an instruction manual for playing on the court, field, or track? While it is good advice for any athlete, 2 Timothy 2:5 is talking about living a life of faith. We can see that by reading the verses around it—check out 2 Timothy 1:3–2:13.

Living a life that is faithful to Christ is not easy. There will be times when you see others cut corners, and you might be tempted to cut them, too. The hardest part is when you see others succeed who haven't played by the rules. You might be somewhere near the middle or at the back of the pack. . .because you played fair. You were being good and faithful to Christ and yet, somehow, you lost.

Don't give up! Continue to live a life of faith, and when it really counts you will receive the victor's crown. Things might not be fair day to day. But if we remain faithful to Christ, He will reward us in heaven.

Thank You, Jesus, for the reminder to be faithful to You! When I am discouraged by others who are cutting corners, keep me strong. I love You, Lord. Amen.

43

Encouragement in the Stories

Everything that was written in the past was written to teach us, so that through the endurance taught in the Scriptures and the encouragement they provide we might have hope.

ROMANS 15:4 NIV

Why should we read God's Word? Let's look at the verse again.

The first reason is *"to teach us."* We learn when we read the Bible. It's an instruction manual, textbook, biography, songbook, and it includes poetry. We can learn about God through what we read.

The second reason is that we get to see the result of what happens when people live through difficult experiences while they follow God. We might think it's not worth following when we're having bad days, but if we read the Bible we find all kinds of people

who discovered that God has always been willing and able to take care of them.

Another reason for spending time with God is finding encouragement in the stories. We all need to be encouraged. You might face a situation that you're sure no one has ever faced. The Bible can prove you've never been alone.

You'll also find hope when you grow closer to God. Stand strong. God will help you through the most difficult days.

Dear God, You want me to spend time with You. I can read more about You. I can also learn what it looks like to really trust You. Help me take time to discover Your stories by reading Your words. Amen.

He Never Disappoints

[God said] "Those who hope in me
will not be disappointed."
ISAIAH 49:23 NIV

Your friend promised to hang out with you after school. He never showed up and he never called. You were excited about a trip at school, but at the last minute it was canceled. You had been waiting to see a movie for a long time, but when you arrived at the theater it was no longer showing.

Disappointment. It's like a lost kitten that keeps following us when we wish it would go home and leave us alone. Our plans are interrupted by disappointment. We struggle to hope when we're disappointed. Trusting others is more difficult when disappointment shows up.

God's Word says, *"Those who hope in me will not be disappointed."* More than anyone you know, God can be trusted. When He says He will do something it's more than a promise, it's a guarantee. He accepts, forgives, loves, provides, brings peace, offers grace, saves, and rewards those who make seeking Him their number-one priority.

Whenever you find yourself disappointed, remember that if God really is the most important priority in your life then the most important part of your life will never disappoint. Hope in Him.

Lord, You want me to see what faithfulness looks like. You've made a lot of promises, and You always keep them. Help me look for hope like a lost treasure. Help me remember I'll always find hope in You. Amen.

Missing the Mark

If we claim we have no sin, we are only fooling ourselves and not living in the truth. But if we confess our sins to him, he is faithful and just to forgive us our sins and to cleanse us from all wickedness.

1 JOHN 1:8–9 NLT

The world is full of good people. There are doctors and teachers, philanthropists and missionaries, volunteers and caregivers. Even saying hi to a new kid in class or helping a neighbor rake leaves are good things. The world is a better place because of them. And if you compare good people to someone like Hitler or Pol Pot (look him up if you don't know him), suddenly they look perfect!

Can you be a good person and still sin? The word *sin* means to miss the mark. . .like at a shooting range. So what mark are you supposed to be hitting? You aren't as bad as most people! The comparison we should be making isn't with other people, but with God. If we aren't as perfect as He is, we have missed the mark—we have sinned. And the truth is we are all sinners. But here's the best news: if we confess our sin, God will forgive us. Not only that, He will wash us completely of anything that is not good if we let Him.

Jesus, it's hard to admit that I'm a sinner. But then I look at Your perfect life, and I know I don't hit the mark. I confess to You. Forgive me. Amen.

God Is for Us

"If God is for us, who can ever be against us?"
ROMANS 8:31 NLT

Some days everything goes wrong. You forget your school project, wake up late, and your dog visits the trash can buffet in the kitchen.

When you get to school you can't find your best friend, you studied the wrong pages for a test, and they're playing a game you hate in PE.

We can be discouraged for many reasons, but when we pay attention to God's Word we discover there isn't any real reason to be frustrated. God is for us.

Think about that for a minute. All the mean things in the world can't stop God from being for us. Nothing anyone can do will stop God from helping us, teaching us, and loving us.

Everyone around us can work overtime to discourage us, but God wrote His words to encourage us. He wants us to be successful, confident, and wise. While He knows we will be discouraged from time to time He wants that discouragement to end the moment we remember some really great news. *God is for us.*

Dear God, when I am discouraged draw me closer to You. My difficult days are no match for Your encouragement. My sadness is an invitation to spend time with You. My moments of frustration give me an opportunity to trust in Your ability to lead. Help me seek Your encouragement today. Amen.

47

Choose Honesty

*Do not lie to each other, since you have taken
off your old self with its practices and have
put on the new self, which is being renewed in
knowledge in the image of its Creator.*
COLOSSIANS 3:9–10 NIV

People have lots of reasons for lying. Maybe they
think a lie will get them out of trouble, or will
save them from getting into trouble. It doesn't matter
why a person decides to lie; God tells us to *stop lying*.

Lying is part of our old self. When we follow God
we learn the value of telling the truth, and honesty
makes a positive difference in how people think of us.

Accepting God's rescue plan means we're new
and different. We help others, share Jesus, and
become more like what God wants us to be.

When we lie we have to remember each story

we tell, but when we tell different stories to different people it's very hard to keep every story straight. Getting caught in a lie makes it harder for other people to trust us.

Make things easier, tell the truth.

Father, You want me to tell the truth, not just some of the time—all the time. I want family and friends to trust me, so help be truthful even if I blow it. Help me be brave enough to always see honesty as the best answer. Amen.

48

Distractions

*I will study your commandments
and reflect on your ways.*
PSALM 119:15 NLT

Maybe you've said something like "God, today I'm going to read Your words, and I'm going to see if I can figure out what they mean." You really want to, but your mind gets distracted, and you can't seem to think clearly.

You remember something you did last week, something you want to do tonight, a favorite television show, or sports team. Your mind can think of almost anything but what you want it to think about. Talk about frustrating.

Distractions are normal. They happen to the best of us. Maybe that's why spending time with God is so important. It helps us learn to think about what He wants us to do. When you make meeting with God as normal as eating lunch you may be surprised at how much you can learn between the distractions.

They may never completely go away, but distractions should never stop you from joining God on the adventure of your life.

Dear God, You never want me to use distractions as an excuse for not spending time with You. The words I read in the Bible are Your words, and You gave them to me so I can be wise in the way I walk with You. I don't want to guess what You want. Help me really get to know You so I can choose Your way. Amen.

49

No Other Name

"For Jesus is the one referred to in the Scriptures, where it says, 'The stone that you builders rejected has now become the cornerstone.' There is salvation in no one else! God has given no other name under heaven by which we must be saved."

Acts 4:11–12 NLT

In churches across the country, missionaries speak about their work around the world. They may have different pictures of different people groups to share, but the message is the same: "These people need to hear about Jesus!"

Why do missionaries care if people in other countries hear about Jesus? Aren't they changing the religion of another culture? And aren't all religions pretty much the same? The Bible says that there is one way to salvation: Jesus Christ. All religions aren't praying to the same God. Christianity is unique in that way.

But Jesus' salvation isn't just for people across an ocean. It's for you and your family and your friends and the neighbor down the street. It's for all of us, right here. So the question is, do you know Jesus' salvation for yourself? Do you know others who need to hear about Jesus? The Bible says that Jesus' disciples were ordinary men. But they had courage to tell others about Christ. You can do that, too!

Jesus, I know that salvation comes only from You. Give me courage to speak to my friends when I feel You asking me to. Give me the right words to say in that moment. Amen.

50

Everyone's Invited

*For in him all things were created: things in
heaven and on earth, visible and invisible,
whether thrones or powers or rulers or
authorities; all things have been created through
him and for him. He is before all things,
and in him all things hold together.*

COLOSSIANS 1:16–17 NIV

In the beginning God created everything and
called it "good." The things we see. The things we
don't see. The things on earth and in heaven. God
made it all.

Nothing can exist without God. He's the only One
who can hold everything together.

God's Word says the only One who is truly good
is God, but because God created all of us not one
of us is better than another. God doesn't look at our

skin color or address. God always looks at our hearts. People with all kinds of skin colors can make good decisions. People with all kinds of skin colors can make bad decisions.

Our choices, not our culture or background, tell the most about who we are. The best news is we're *all* invited to follow God.

God, You want me to understand that even though someone is different from me You still love them. All of us have a choice to follow You, but none of us has a choice about where we're born or the color of our skin. Help me remember that all people can love You, and You love all people. Amen.

51

Curious Enough to Keep Asking

*If you need wisdom, ask our generous God,
and he will give it to you. He will not rebuke you
for asking. But when you ask him, be sure that
your faith is in God alone.*

JAMES 1:5–6 NLT

Why did God give us the Bible? He knew we
would have questions. God isn't upset when
we ask questions, but He wants us to trust Him even
if we don't like the answer.

Many people ask questions about why God does
what He does, but they don't really want an answer.
Their questions can show that they don't trust God,
or that they are trying to make others doubt Him.

God's answers always help make our faith stronger.

It's easy to doubt when you've never seen
something with your own eyes. This is why faith is

important. Faith is being able to believe something is true and trustworthy without seeing it first.

Ask questions and then open the Bible. That's where you'll find answers. When you don't read God's Word it can be easy to be confused.

When we have doubts, faith steps in and believes God can make us wise enough to understand, patient enough to wait, and curious enough to keep asking.

Father, You don't want me to be confused or ask questions I don't want You to answer. You want me to trust You to answer and to believe that Your answers are perfect. Help me accept Your answers. Amen.

52

A Servant's Heart

"Then those that are right with God will say, 'Lord, when did we see You hungry and feed You? When did we see You thirsty and give You a drink? When did we see You a stranger and give You a room? When did we see You had no clothes and we gave You clothes? And when did we see You sick or in prison and we came to You?' Then the King will say, 'For sure, I tell you, because you did it to one of the least of My brothers, you have done it to Me.'"

MATTHEW 25:37–40 NLV

The Bible talks about the hungry, the thirsty, the stranger, the person in need of clothes, the sick, and the prisoner. There have been a lot of good ministries started just for these people. Many churches support these ministries with money. Other churches send volunteers. But how often do we really see the hurting and helpless around us?

Standing up for a classmate who is being bullied, sitting with a new student at lunch, helping your little sister after she falls off her bike: these are all ways of offering God's love to those around us. Having a servant's heart means noticing "the least of these" and acting on it.

Jesus, I want to serve You. I want to be able to see others with Your eyes. Give me the courage to help when I see someone in need. Thank You for being the example of a servant to me. Amen.

Serious Encouragement

Let us consider how we may spur one another on toward love and good deeds.

HEBREWS 10:24 NIV

We all have friends who want to hang out, play a video game, watch a movie, or get a soda. Not many of us have friends ask if we want to help mow a neighbor's lawn, serve in a soup kitchen, help with younger children, or visit a nursing home.

God's Word says we should seriously think about ways we can encourage other Christians to love people and find ways to help them.

We often think that after we have put in our time at school, doing chores, sleeping, and eating, the rest of our time is available for us to do the things we like to do. If God is who we follow, He needs to be in charge of *all* areas of our lives—not just the ones we

allow Him to control.

It may sound strange, but when we follow God we can encourage others by finding new ways to do what Jesus would do. We get to use our hands, feet, words, and money to honor God and serve the people He loves.

Dear God, You want me to serve, but also encourage others to serve. One of the best reasons to serve is to show how much You can change the way I do things. Help me be creative in serving You well. Amen.

54

The Puppy outside the Zoo

*Don't envy sinners,
but always continue to fear the LORD.*
PROVERBS 23:17 NLT

Imagine planning to visit an amazing zoo. You dream for days about what it'll be like to see lions, tigers, bears, and other animals with names you can't pronounce. On the way into the zoo you see someone with a puppy. Would you give up a trip to the zoo to play with a puppy?

This should be an easy choice, but you need to remember that sometimes we give up God's best by trying to do things that people who don't know Jesus might do. When the Bible talks about envy it means we want what someone else has. When we envy sinners we're saying that we want the things God has told us we don't need, He doesn't want us to have, and

will cause us to disobey Him.

When we're told to "continue to fear the Lord," we're asked to understand there's nothing and no one more awesome than God. When we stop paying attention to God we begin to think that other stuff might be more awesome. When we make this choice it's like playing with a puppy outside the zoo. Never settle for less than God.

God, help me never think that anything can compare to how awesome You are. Help me remember that when I sin I'm saying I don't think You know what's best for me. Help me always trust in You. Amen.

55

They Play on Our Team

There is neither Jew nor Gentile, neither slave nor free, nor is there male and female, for you are all one in Christ Jesus.
GALATIANS 3:28 NIV

Y ou go to church with people you know. You sing with them every weekend and go to school with some of them during the week. You can feel really comfortable at your church, and that's a good thing.

Now, think about what it would be like to bring Christians from every nation you can think of and put them in the same building for a weekend church service. How comfortable would you feel?

Sometimes we may think the only Christians we can trust and talk to are those who go to our church or school. We're comfortable with the people who live on our block or play on our team.

Our verse is saying something like "There isn't eagle, bear, buffalo, or ram. There isn't Asian, Caucasian, African American, or Spanish. We work for one team—God's."

Sometimes we don't act like it, but those are the rules according to God's playbook. He never wants divisions between people. He gave us a plan to be united. That should happen when anyone accepts God's rescue plan of salvation.

Heavenly Father, You've always wanted me to know I'm not the only one who wants to serve You. There are many people I've never met who love You. Help me love all the other people who love You. Amen.

56

Sleep Tight

*My child, don't lose sight of common sense
and discernment. Hang on to them, for they
will refresh your soul. They are like jewels on a
necklace. They keep you safe on your way,
and your feet will not stumble. You can go to bed
without fear; you will lie down and sleep soundly.*
PROVERBS 3:21–24 NLT

When you were little, were you ever afraid of
the boogeyman? As you've grown, do you get
scared about bad things that happen in the world?

King Solomon, the wisest man who ever lived,
wrote the book of Proverbs to his son. When we read
it, it's like we're listening to a conversation. Think
about it this way: Solomon has his arm over his son's
shoulder and is sharing the secrets of life that God
has revealed to him. Sometimes a thought comes to

mind and he blurts it out, so we get some choppy-sounding proverbs. Other times he is trying to describe something like wisdom, so he talks about it more emotionally.

In these verses, the king is urging his son to hang on to wisdom. Being wise will keep his son safe because wise decisions will keep him from getting tripped up. It's the same for us today. You don't have to be scared of the bogeyman. Learn the wisdom of scripture, and sleep tight.

God, help me make wise decisions so that I don't get tripped up. Take away my fears. Amen.

57

Easier to Blame

*Then the LORD God asked the woman,
"What have you done?" "The serpent deceived me,"
she replied. "That's why I ate it."*

GENESIS 3:13 NLT

We all sin. God told us we would. Sometimes we
don't want to admit it.

It's easier to blame others. Maybe you want to
blame a family member who made you mad or a
teacher who gave more homework than you thought
was fair.

When the first man and woman (Adam and Eve)
committed the first sin, they didn't search for God
and apologize. They didn't ask for forgiveness. They
didn't even admit what they'd done. Adam blamed
Eve for giving him a piece of fruit from the forbidden
tree, and Eve blamed the serpent for being deceitful.

Men, women, boys, and girls have been blaming one another ever since.

All of us can come up with an excuse for our sin. God never accepts excuses, but He does offer forgiveness when we admit we're wrong.

It's hard to be friends with God when we refuse to be honest with Him. Sometimes we forget He already knows what we do. Trying to hide or blaming others never works.

Dear God, You want me to be honest with You. I should never blame anyone for the poor choices I make. My sin is a reason to pray right away so I can be forgiven, and You can help me make better choices. Help me remember to always be honest with You. Amen.

58

Trading Failure for Success

[Jesus said], "My grace is all you need. My power works best in weakness." So now I am glad to boast about my weaknesses, so that the power of Christ can work through me.

2 CORINTHIANS 12:9 NLT

God knows everything. We know only what we learn. Sometimes we learn through mistakes.

Sin is always failure, but failure isn't always sin. Doing something God tells us not to do is sin. Trying something that just doesn't work out is failure. But we don't have to learn everything through trial and error because God already gave us His commands, so we don't really have an excuse for not learning them.

God knows we will fail, so He shows His power through forgiveness of our sins and encouragement in our failures.

The things we can't do on our own are things that God has no trouble doing. When we're weak we shouldn't be surprised to see how God's strength can accomplish what we can't.

As Christians we're part of God's family. As part of God's family we can talk to God about anything. He wants to teach us through our failures and to help us in our weakness. He loves turning failure into success.

Lord, You want me to be a student who learns from You and accepts Your help when I fail. Help me remember I never have to hide from You. Your lessons aren't always easy, but they help me find my place in Your plan and discover Your strength in my weakness. Amen.

59

Music

*Each tree is recognized by its own fruit.
People do not pick figs from thornbushes, or grapes
from briers. A good man brings good things out of
the good stored up in his heart, and an evil man
brings evil things out of the evil stored up in his heart.
For the mouth speaks what the heart is full of.*

LUKE 6:44–45 NIV

Since the dawn of time, humans have had a
connection with music. It's a deeply personal
form of communication that reaches to our very core.

Regardless of the type of music that draws you,
you should take an honest look at it. The Bible says,
"Each tree is recognized by its own fruit." If music
is the tree, then the words are the fruit. What are the
words communicating? Are they consistent with
what is found in the Bible? When you listen to music,

you are storing up things in your heart...either good or evil. There is no right or wrong kind of music. All genres of music have good and bad songs...even praise music! It's up to you to decide if they line up with what the Bible teaches. That takes effort on your part. It's an important challenge because the Bible says, "For the mouth speaks what the heart is full of."

Lord, I like music. I want to honor You with it. Remind me to take the time to listen to the words I'm singing. Give me the courage and the willpower to change my playlist. Amen.

Getting Ready for the Next Phase

[Jesus said] "Whoever can be trusted with very little can also be trusted with much, and whoever is dishonest with very little will also be dishonest with much."

LUKE 16:10 NIV

God is looking for faithful guys your age. His plan for their future is amazing, but He knows they'll need training for the next phase of their adventure.

Imagine if God were to say to you, "I have something only you can do and I want you to start training today so you'll be ready."

You'd probably get excited. God has a plan, and He wants you to be ready. "What do You want me to do, God?" you ask.

"Obey your parents and clean your room" is the reply.

Wait! What does that story have to do with God's plan? God often asks us to do simple, but less exciting things to see if we'll be faithful in doing our best. We learn patience, obedience, and faithfulness when we do small things well.

If we can be trusted with small things we can be trusted with bigger things. If we can't be trusted to take care of the small things God might need to wait until we are trustworthy to show us the next step in His training plans for us.

Dear God, You want me to be a trusted example of someone who really follows You. Help me obey even when I think I'm ready for more responsibility. Amen.

61

Perfectly Designed

Thank you for making me so wonderfully complex! Your workmanship is marvelous—how well I know it.
PSALM 139:14 NLT

Joints allow fingers and toes to move. Your eyes let you see colors, textures, and the faces of people you know. Your ears allow you to hear music, voices, and nature.

Our bodies are the result of a loving God who knew we would need fingers that bend in order to hold a cup of water, brains that understand color, and ears inspired by sound.

God crafted you into a marvelous creation that is extremely complex and perfectly designed.

The psalm writer shows us that thanking God is a great way to respond when we think about the way

God made us, even when we don't think we're perfect because we see something about ourselves we don't like, or when accident, injury, or disease makes us feel less than perfect. Our bodies aren't forever, but our souls can live with God for eternity. As amazing as our bodies are, God is more interested in the condition of our souls. When we thank God for the creation of our bodies it indicates our souls are in pretty good shape.

Father, You want me to be thankful for the way You created me. Help me see the amazing parts of how You created me. I know that when You gave me life You gave me a future. Amen.

62

Don't Delay!

I will hasten and not delay to obey your commands.
PSALM 119:60 NIV

When you disobey your parents it doesn't take long for you to discover that obedience would have had a much better outcome than the cost for poor choices. God blesses right living, but when we sin against God's commands there are consequences.

When we obey we'll discover that we're satisfied with our decisions. We don't have to second-guess whether we made the right choice. God's assurance that we are doing the right thing makes it easier to obey without spending too much time thinking about a different choice.

Every choice we make is part of the lifelong race we run, and making the best choices allows us to finish the race strong.

We shouldn't say, "Maybe tomorrow" when it comes to obeying God, either. The longer we delay, the harder it is to make the right decision. We are tempted to compromise, which leads to a choice that isn't exactly what God asked us to do.

When you know the right thing to do there is never a good reason for you to delay obedience.

Jesus, You want me to decide that obeying You is more important than trying to find a way out of it. Help me accept that I'm broken inside when I disobey and that You're the only One who can repair the brokenness that keeps me from obeying You completely. Amen.

63

Discovering God

And God said to Moses, "I AM WHO I AM."
And He said, "Say to the Israelites, 'I AM has sent me
to you.'"... This is My name forever. By this name
I am to be remembered by all people for all time.
EXODUS 3:14–15 NLV

Aiden was a fun kid in his youth group. He was always good for a laugh, and his jokes were never at the expense of others, either. One week the leader asked, "When you think about God, what picture comes to mind?" The kids gave all kinds of answers. Some thought of God as a bright light. Others saw Him as a king sitting on a throne. A few saw Him as an old man. Then Aiden's hand went up. Everyone expected Aiden to give a silly answer, but instead he said, "When I think about God, I see Him standing behind a big sheet. At first, all I can see are

His hands and feet sticking out, because He is bigger than the sheet. That's all I know about Him at first. But then I come to church and I learn more about God, so the sheet is pulled back just a little. I read my Bible and the more I learn, the more the sheet is pulled back."

Jump back several thousand years. Moses is on his way to tell the Israelites about God. But what if they don't accept him? So God pulls away part of the sheet. He tells Moses His personal name. God wanted His people to know that He was present for them, and forever. Wow! God wants you to know Him personally, too. What are you waiting for?

Lord, I want to know more about You. Thank You for caring for me so much that You would choose to tell me more about You. Amen.

64

The Right Steps

We can make our plans, but the LORD determines our steps.
PROVERBS 16:9 NLT

You might have a career in the back of your mind that you're planning to go into when you finish school. You might be thinking of a college, a trade school, or a whole lot of training.

It's possible all you're really thinking about is what you'll have at your next meal, if you can beat your high score on a game you like, or how late you'll get to stay up when you're older.

We all have plans, and we're pretty certain we can make them happen, but the simple act of living can change our plans. We can adjust and adapt to the best of our ability, but even that may not be enough.

Our best decision will be to let God change our

plans if He wants.

God knows everything about you. He knows your future and doesn't want you to struggle to figure it out. If we can accept that God's plan is much better than ours it will be easier to let Him help us take the right next steps.

Heavenly Father, You want me to plan all I want, and then let You adjust my plan so I can always follow You instead of trying to find You after I have run away from You. Help my steps forward follow the map You've made for me. Amen.

65

Joy Inspired

*The generous will prosper; those who refresh
others will themselves be refreshed.*
PROVERBS 11:25 NLT

Adults buy investments because they want to
earn more than they spend. They save in order
to keep more than they had. They're careful about
what they buy because they don't want to be wasteful.

God's Word says that when people are generous they
prosper, but how can you prosper when you give away
something without expecting something in return?

Giving to others builds relationships. When you
help others there's a good chance they won't forget
your kindness. Instead of money being your focus
you invest in friendships that will last long after the
money is gone.

There's no price on the value of people who care

about you. You can't buy it, beg for it, or think you'll always have it.

The generous prosper because they understand money doesn't deliver joy, but joy can be recognized in a generous heart. We give because we've received. We share because someone shared with us. We love because God loved us.

Generous people stand out to those who are used to seeing selfishness. They are remembered. They are given gratitude. They rarely regret their own generosity.

Dear God, You want me to be generous. You want my generosity to help other people, but also to keep me from selfishness. Help me give because other people have needs, and because I learned giving from You. Amen.

66

Bullies

Saul said to David, "You are not able to go and fight against this Philistine. You are only a young man, while he has been a man of war since he was young." But David said to Saul..."The Lord Who saved me from the foot of the lion and from the foot of the bear, will save me from the hand of this Philistine."

1 Samuel 17:33–34, 37 NLV

Bullies come in all shapes and sizes. The Bible's most famous bully is Goliath, a nine-foot-nine-inch tall Philistine. Each day, he taunted the Israelites to send their best warrior to fight him. Whoever was left standing would win the war. The Israelites were shaking in their boots! No one wanted to fight him. Then David, who was too young to be a soldier, showed up with food for his older brothers. David knew that it was God who had been insulted, not man. So it would be God standing up against the bully through David. . .and God is much bigger than Goliath!

You don't always have to get in the middle of a fight to fight a bully. Like David, realize that God is bigger than any bully. Befriend those who are picked on. Kindness can go a long way.

God, remind me of all the times You fought for me so that I will be confident when I come up against a bully. Give me courage to make friends with kids who are being picked on. Amen.

67

Controlled Strength

Let's not merely say that we love each other; let us show the truth by our actions.

1 JOHN 3:18 NLT

Maybe you've been told to act like a gentleman. Perhaps you thought that meant to act like a man who is weak, so you stayed quiet and didn't talk to anyone.

When you understand what being a gentleman really is you might have a different opinion about what you're supposed to do in order to show this quality to others.

Being a gentleman doesn't mean to intentionally show weakness. When you're asked to be a gentleman you should remember that God gave you many great strengths. There are things you're really good at. Being a guy is an active adventurous job, but being a gentleman doesn't mean you try to deny all the things that make you who you are. The best description of being a gentleman is *controlled strength*.

Think about a car. It has an accelerator that makes the car move. Like that car, a gentleman moves carefully so he doesn't overpower conversations, games, or situations. He remains strong, but in control. No matter the occasion it's always a good decision to be a gentleman.

Lord, You want me to use every good quality I have, but You want me to keep those strengths controlled. Jesus did that when He walked the earth. Help me be a gentleman who controls his responses and actions. Amen.

68

In Search of Wise Guys

The wisdom that comes from heaven is first of all pure; then peace-loving, considerate, submissive, full of mercy and good fruit, impartial and sincere.

JAMES 3:17 NIV

You want to be wise, right? You want God to help you learn things you should know, respond to others in a way that honors God, and give proof that you're walking with the One who rescued you.

God's wisdom is pure. It's not influenced by hatred, revenge, or anger. It's a perfect model to follow.

God's wisdom is peace-loving, which means it's not interested in battle, but in demonstrating qualities of peaceful solution.

God's wisdom is considerate because it seeks to honor others.

God's wisdom is submissive and pays attention to

the whole story.

God's wisdom is merciful and offers forgiveness.

God's wisdom is impartial and never makes decisions based on where you live or your cultural background.

God's wisdom is sincere and never deceitful.

You might want God's wisdom for yourself. His wisdom pays attention to what God has already said and subtracts emotions from issues, so when a decision is made it's fair because all sides have been considered.

Dear God, You want me to show wisdom in my decisions. It seems easier to make a decision and apologize later, but You want me to be wise before I make a decision. Help me be patient enough to think through each issue. Amen.

69

Godliness Conditioning

"Physical training is good, but training for godliness is much better, promising benefits in this life and in the life to come."

1 TIMOTHY 4:8 NLT

You may attend a strength and conditioning class in school or maybe PE. You might like to run, play sports, or swim. This kind of training usually makes you feel good.

When you go out for sports you have many practices to attend, games to play, and you have to get in shape so you're prepared.

The apostle Paul said this kind of training is a good thing. When he was alive the big sports were foot races or track and field games. People understood that practice was needed for these races, and they admired those who trained hard.

Paul said the same commitment to living God's way was even better. Why? The benefit of this training is helpful while we live on earth and when we get to heaven.

What if we put as much time and effort into living God's way as we do in preparing for sports?

Letting God work through us could change the world.

Lord, You have a workout plan for my soul, and You want me to train. Help me take the time, expend the energy, get in shape, and learn from the best. May the things I learn help those who need You. Amen.

70

Lessons in Learning

At that time the disciples came to Jesus and asked, "Who, then, is the greatest in the kingdom of heaven?" He called a little child to him, and placed the child among them. And he said: "...whoever takes the lowly position of this child is the greatest in the kingdom of heaven."

MATTHEW 18:1–4 NIV

In Jesus' day, children began learning certain passages of scripture as early as three years old. They began reading the Bible between the ages of five and six. They learned the Mishnah at ten and studied the Talmud at fifteen. Children were in a constant state of learning. None of them felt as though they could stand beside their teacher and begin to lead the class. So when the disciples began to argue with one another and say, "Who, then, is

the greatest in the kingdom of heaven?" they were fighting for a position of leadership.

Spiritual training takes a lifetime. Do you want to be great in the kingdom of heaven? Don't imagine you know as much or more than your teachers. Humble yourself. Be like the children in Jesus' day... in a constant state of learning.

God, I like for others to know how smart I am. It really hurts to admit when I don't know something. But that's what You said I have to do if I want to be great in Your kingdom. Help me be humble, always discovering new things. Amen.

71

Secrets Betrayed

*A gossip betrays a confidence; so avoid anyone
who talks too much.*
PROVERBS 20:19 NIV

People have to trust you when sharing something
they wouldn't tell anyone else.

Imagine being sworn to secrecy. You solemnly
promise silence. The secret is told and your friend
leaves believing their confidence is safe. As far as
you're concerned it *is* safe. You have no plans to tell
anyone.

However, the more you think about it the more
impressive and powerful the secret becomes. You
know something no one else knows. Suddenly you're
considering the idea of sharing the secret. The harder
you try to stop it the more it wants to come out.

When the words finally tumble from your lips to

other ears you think the only way to minimize the damage is to swear that person to secrecy, but the cycle is set to reboot and start all over again with worse results.

The Bible tells us to stop gossiping, and then it tells us to stay away from people who gossip.

A gossip betrays another person, spreads information that may not be true, and can hurt the person who trusted them with their secret.

Dear God, You want me to be a trustworthy friend. Help me refuse to gossip. If I'm concerned for my friend give me the courage to talk to an adult, but never another friend. Help me pray for those who trust me because I can always talk to You about anything. Amen.

72

For the God Who Has Everything

*Acknowledge that the LORD is God! He made us,
and we are his. We are his people, the sheep of
his pasture. Enter his gates with thanksgiving;
go into his courts with praise. Give thanks
to him and praise his name.*
PSALM 100:3–4 NLT

At the very center of gratitude is the understanding that someone is more important than we are. We can't thank someone without recognizing they did something for us that we couldn't do for ourselves no matter how hard we tried.

In order to show gratitude to God we have to acknowledge that He is God. We admit that He made us and takes care of us.

This is why we sing songs of praise and worship

in church. We tell God in song that we're His people and we're grateful for everything He does. We see all the beautiful things He created, and it's impressive enough that we can't help but worship Him. Even His name is so honorable that we should never use it in a dishonorable way.

We have always been important to God. Maybe a good question is, "How important is God to us?"

God, there is nothing You have done for me that I could have done myself. You gave me life, offered rescue, forgiveness, and grace. You share Your creation with me. You give me courage, hope, and love. I'm yours. You're mine. I am grateful that You're greater. Amen.

73

Talking with God

*"Go out and stand before me on the mountain,"
the LORD told him. And as Elijah stood there,
the LORD passed by, and a mighty windstorm
hit the mountain. It was such a terrible blast
that the rocks were torn loose, but the LORD
was not in the wind. After the wind there was
an earthquake, but the LORD was not in the
earthquake. And after the earthquake there was
a fire, but the LORD was not in the fire. And after
the fire there was the sound of a gentle whisper.*

1 KINGS 19:11–12 NLT

ave you ever been angry with God? I mean, really
angry? Things in your life might not be going the
way you want and you wonder where God is!

The Bible tells us about a man named Elijah.
He was a prophet of God and had just been used

to perform a mighty miracle. But now the king's wife had put a hit out on his life. Elijah runs scared, and hides. Eventually God tells him to stand on a mountain. There are powerful winds, an earthquake, and a fire, but that wasn't God. God began to speak in a gentle whisper.

Sometimes we expect God to rescue us with a big, thunderous show of strength. Our talking to God becomes a list of wants or demands. It's okay to tell God how we are feeling. Elijah did. But we need to wait and listen for the gentle whisper of God.

Heavenly Father, thank You for caring about what I'm going through. Help me to seek You in silence. I'm listening, Lord! Amen.

Trusted to Take Care

*Keep your lives free from the love of money and be
content with what you have, because God has said,
"Never will I leave you; never will I forsake you."*
HEBREWS 13:5 NIV

For a Christian to be greedy is like saying, "God,
I know You made the planets, stars, and space.
I know You created water, rocks, and sky. You did
an impressive job creating fish, animals, and birds.
However, I'm not really sure You can be trusted to
take care of me."

Money is useful. It's important in taking care
of a family, paying bills, and buying gifts. Money
is also something that can be worshipped. We can
love money, want a growing collection of currency,
and look for all kinds of ways to get more. In really
bad cases we forget the important things in life. Our

families become less important, helping others is rare, and sharing our money is nearly impossible.

God wants us to like what we have, share what we've got, and live like He's the only One we really need, because in the end we'll find satisfaction, giving, and trusting are all things that help us see His love more clearly.

Jesus, You want me to believe You can and will take care of me. When I'm greedy I show that I don't think You can be trusted. Help me be satisfied with Your gifts, impressed by Your help, and overwhelmed by Your love. Amen.

75

A Clear Voice

The LORD says, "I will guide you along the best pathway
for your life. I will advise you and watch over you."
PSALM 32:8 NLT

ew cars have computer mapping programs
known as GPS. They speak in a pleasant voice
advising you to turn left, turn right, make a U-turn,
when you've arrived, if you need to recalculate, and to
let you know if it doesn't understand you.

One man used his GPS to get to a friend's house.
He'd never been there before and listened closely
for directions. The GPS unit told him to turn left. He
turned and wound up in the middle of a field.

As trustworthy as GPS might be, God's never
been wrong about the path you should take. His Word
tells us where to go, and He always watches over us.

We may not hear a pleasant voice say, "Turn left

and find a man who needs to know more about Me,"
but His Word tells us there are many who need to
know what we're learning. His voice is heard most
clearly in the words of the Bible. Read daily, and avoid
confusion.

Dear God, You don't want me to be confused.
You guide, and if I'm paying attention I follow.
Help me see Your words as direction for my life,
hope for my soul, and wisdom for my journey.
Help me love You enough to follow. Help me follow
You enough to make it habit. Amen.

76

Life: Out of Balance

*You say, "I am allowed to do anything"—but not
everything is good for you. And even though
"I am allowed to do anything," I must
not become a slave to anything.*

1 CORINTHIANS 6:12 NLT

When your family wants you to have a *balanced*
meal you're probably going to get more
than one type of food. Veggies and fruit will make
an appearance, but there may be other foods that
complete the meal. You'd probably get tired of a diet
made entirely of bread, juice, or even snack cakes.

God gave us many things to enjoy, but when
we do just one thing then our lives can get out of
balance. We can eat lots of different things, so you
don't have to settle for onion skins and lime soda.

We should also balance the activities we're

involved in, including our screen time. Anything that makes us think or do something that seems more important than following God tips us off balance.

When we keep doing things that lead us further from God, they can become habits that are hard to break and don't allow God to offer wisdom.

Lord, You made so many things I get to enjoy.
Help me discover beauty in Your creation.
Help me notice when I'm paying too much
attention to something that captures my thoughts,
making it hard to listen to You. Amen.

77

God Made Me Uh-mayzin!

For you created my inmost being; you knit me together in my mother's womb. I praise you because I am fearfully and wonderfully made; your works are wonderful, I know that full well. My frame was not hidden from you when I was made in the secret place, when I was woven together in the depths of the earth. Your eyes saw my unformed body; all the days ordained for me were written in your book before one of them came to be.

PSALM 139:13–16 NIV

Do you have a little brother or sister? Or maybe a younger cousin or kids in your neighborhood? Maybe excited moms and dads have shown pictures of them as babies, or even before they were born!

God didn't stop creating with Adam and Eve. Every child is a picture of God's hand at work. And what's true about others is true about you, too. You were knit together by the hand of God. Imagine that! The Bible says, "I praise you because I am fearfully and wonderfully made." The words *fearfully and wonderfully made* mean "an awesome and distinct work." That's what you are! There is no one else like you, and God made you awesome!

Thank You, God, for creating me.
I am an awesome work of Yours! Help me to
always remember that and praise You for it. Amen.

78

Hatred in Disguise?

People may cover their hatred with pleasant words, but they're deceiving you. They pretend to be kind, but don't believe them. Their hearts are full of many evils. While their hatred may be concealed by trickery, their wrongdoing will be exposed in public.

PROVERBS 26:24–26 NLT

Have you ever had someone hate you with kindness? Usually if someone doesn't like you they let you, and everyone else, know. They don't hide hatred.

The people who hate, but act like they don't, think they have you fooled. They usually don't. It could be a look in their eye, a firm line on their face, or the way they speak. All the time they may be trying to figure out how to seek revenge for whatever they think you've done to them.

You could try talking to them to find out what's wrong, but this person may continue acting as if everything is perfect. The last thing you want to do is intentionally make them upset. God wants us to live at peace with everyone if possible. Sometimes it isn't feasible, but always seek peace first.

Dear God, You want me to know hatred is an emotion to avoid. Hatred is like fire to a piece of wood. It keeps burning until there's nothing left but ashes. Hatred consumes a person, and others can see it happen. Your best answer to hatred is forgiveness and love. Help me take Your best choice. Amen.

79

Bad Days

*The righteous cry out, and the LORD hears them;
he delivers them from all their troubles.
The LORD is close to the brokenhearted and saves
those who are crushed in spirit. The righteous
person may have many troubles, but the LORD
delivers him from them all.*

PSALM 34:17–19 NIV

f Christians have bad days, too, what makes a Christian's life better than the lives of those who don't follow Jesus?

God's Word is filled with people who had very bad days. Daniel spent time with lions, David was chased by Saul, Moses lived with complainers, and Joseph's brothers sold him as a slave.

In each story these guys took their bad days and talked to God about them. God rescued them from the impact of bad days. This didn't mean they never had trouble, but when they did God gave them everything they needed to face hard times.

God stays close to those who feel like they've been stepped on. He listens. He rescues. He loves.

Is serving God better than refusing rescue? Daniel, David, Moses, and Joseph thought so.

Heavenly Father, You want me to know that when things seem hopeless You can rescue me. Your words say, "The righteous person may have many troubles, but the LORD delivers him from them all." Sometimes You give me the answer, but sometimes You give me the strength to live through bad days. Thanks for thinking enough of me to help me through days I never wanted to face. Amen.

80

Show Some Respect

For you are free, yet you are God's slaves,
so don't use your freedom as an excuse to do evil.
Respect everyone, and love the family of believers.
Fear God, and respect the king.
1 PETER 2:16–18 NLT

Tim's coach was gone for the day and left the
assistant coach in charge of team practice. The
team always started with stretches and warm-ups.
As Tim and the other kids were finishing the jumping
jacks, they heard a voice thundering out, "Again!"
A bit confused, they went through the jumping jacks
a second time. Just as they were almost done the
coach shouted, "Again!" When some of the kids asked
why, the coach said, "You're sloppy! Your hands need
to clap together and your legs need to be out, forming
an A." Tim was frustrated and angry. On the fourth

time to go through the jumping jacks, he smacked his hands together and stomped his feet on the floor. Several teammates started laughing at his antics. But it also humiliated his coach.

On the surface, Tim was doing exactly what the coach was asking, right? But everyone saw through to the motive. It was filled with a bad attitude.

Obedience can be tough, but God tells us to respect and submit to leaders in our lives. Tim chose to let anger override his fear of God. But you don't have to! Choose to obey.

God, I want to respect my teachers and coaches. Sometimes it's hard to do, but Your words are clear. Help me obey! Amen.

81

Listen Up

[God] gives grace generously. As the Scriptures say, "God opposes the proud but gives grace to the humble."

JAMES 4:6 NLT

Maybe you're a guy who can take a loaf of bread, a piece of drawing paper, a stapler, and two stamps and figure out a way to solve world hunger. You're smart and come up with some impressive solutions.

Maybe you're a guy who can fix things. Computer issues aren't a challenge to you. Your family and friends call on you to troubleshoot problems, and you take care of them.

When you are really good at something you can begin to think that maybe you're smart enough to figure out life's biggest problems on your own. When other people struggle you have answers.

The problem is, you'll never be God. As smart and resourceful as you may be you don't have all the answers. You need God as much as anyone else. You always have more to learn.

Seek humility, honor God, and pay attention. He's got some great things to teach when we listen.

Dear God, You don't want me to think I have all the answers. It's a good thing to be smart and to help others. It's an incredible thing to know the God who created wisdom. Help me always seek You and ask for Your help even when I think I already have a solution. Your way is perfect, and I become wise when I ask for help. Amen.

82

Rescued

There is no difference between Jew and Gentile, for all have sinned and fall short of the glory of God, and all are justified freely by his grace through the redemption that came by Christ Jesus.

ROMANS 3:22–24 NIV

You've probably heard that we don't measure up to God's standard of perfection. Breaking one of God's laws is no different from breaking them all. One sin proves you aren't perfect, and God can only accept perfection.

It doesn't matter where you're from, either. No one gets special privileges. Everyone blows it, and God knows it.

Things can seem hopeless. It feels like we're doomed. It seems that no matter what we do God will never be pleased.

God's Son, Jesus, came to earth to live with humans, but for the first time there was someone who *was* perfect. He never sinned. He never fell short. He never broke God's law. And He loved us.

Jesus was on a rescue mission. When He died on the cross He was the perfect sacrifice. He made it possible for God to see those who followed Him as perfect. He rose from the dead so that when we come up short Jesus can make things right.

Father, You gave Your best gift so I could talk to You. Thanks for sending Jesus to rescue me. Accepting Your best gift of rescue has changed my life, left me in awe, and given me a reason to be grateful. Amen.

83

Who's Carrying Your Burdens?

Jesus said, "Come to me, all of you who are weary and carry heavy burdens, and I will give you rest."

MATTHEW 11:28 NLT

D o you have good self-esteem? Some people are concerned that others don't feel like they really matter, so they try to help these people feel better about themselves. They don't want to see anyone left out, so they work hard to include everyone.

God's Word shares examples of people who weren't included, often left alone, and who struggled with how to handle the troubles they faced.

Jesus told those who would listen that He knew they were carrying burdens. He knew things seemed impossible. Jesus told them to come to Him. He wanted to hear about their struggles. He was willing to listen. After hearing them He offered to give them rest by taking their burdens for them.

We'll always feel better about ourselves when God's love is placed deeply in our hearts. He loves you enough to listen and can be trusted to take good care of your heaviest burdens.

In the end it shouldn't surprise us when we value God more than ourselves and then reach out to share His good news with others.

Lord, You want me to trust that You care enough about me to pay attention to the things that bother me. Thanks for listening and for being willing to take my burden. Help me be open to giving my hardest struggles to You. Amen.

84

Video Games

Christian brothers, keep your minds thinking about whatever is true, whatever is respected, whatever is right, whatever is pure, whatever can be loved, and whatever is well thought of. If there is anything good and worth giving thanks for, think about these things.

PHILIPPIANS 4:8 NLV

Adam loved video games. He had a PS4 and a Wii, but what he really wanted was an Xbox, like his friends. His parents told him if he worked and earned the money for it himself, he could buy it. He did odd jobs for anyone who would hire him and saved for several months. Finally the day came for him to go buy the system. He was excited! He couldn't wait to buy some games to play on his new Xbox.

Are you like Adam? Do you like playing video games? How do you pick what games you play—and which ones you don't? There are so many games out there: from childish to violent and everything in between. Sometimes it's hard to know where to draw the line for ourselves.

The Bible gives us a guideline to follow: fill your mind with whatever is true, right, and pure. If our thoughts turn away from whatever is good as we play video games, it's time to rethink the game.

God, thank You for guidelines on what I should fill my head with. Help me to choose my games wisely. Amen.

85

The Need to Intercede

I urge, then, first of all, that petitions, prayers, intercession and thanksgiving be made for all people—for kings and all those in authority, that we may live peaceful and quiet lives in all godliness and holiness. This is good, and pleases God our Savior, who wants all people to be saved and to come to a knowledge of the truth.

1 TIMOTHY 2:1–4 NIV

Puggles was a stray dog that found Manuel. The dog was hungry, so Manuel gave him a bite of his sandwich. That was the beginning of their friendship. Manuel had always wanted a dog, but his family insisted that he put posters up to see if Puggles was someone's missing pet. No one came to claim the dog, and with each passing day their friendship grew.

One day Manuel stepped up and interceded for Puggles. Manuel shared all the reasons why Puggles should find a home with his family.

God also wants us to intercede for others. We stand up in support of them when we pray to God for and about them. When people can't pray maybe we're supposed to.

Dear God, You want me to intercede for others when they can't pray for themselves. Help me show love by asking You to help them. I should intercede for people who are sick as well as those who need to know You. Help me care enough about others to intercede. Amen.

86

Faithful in the Doing

Lazy people want much but get little, but those who work hard will prosper.

PROVERBS 13:4 NLT

Some people are afraid of hard work. They find an excuse for every request for work. They have big dreams about nice things, but it's doing *work* that bothers them.

People who might be described as lazy aren't just those who like rest. They might actually be very active, but the things they do are efforts designed to get them out of work. They never seem to have enough, but never want to work.

God's Word tells us that people who work hard prosper. They may not have a lot of money, but they know that work is what allows them to show honor to their families, provide for others, and contribute to

making their community better.

Hard work also provides hope. When you work you learn things that help you see a bright future. Hard work can be found in classrooms, living rooms, and weight rooms.

God often brings better responsibilities when we are faithful in what we're already doing. Don't give up. Do your best. Be satisfied in the work you can do.

Lord, You want me to value hard work because work helps me become satisfied, it helps my family, and it gives me the chance to help those who need help. I don't want to complain about work, so help me choose a good attitude as I serve others. Amen.

87

Resist the Devil

So humble yourselves before God.
Resist the devil, and he will flee from you.
Come close to God, and God will come close to you.
Wash your hands, you sinners; purify your hearts,
for your loyalty is divided between God and the world.

JAMES 4:7–8 NLT

Each year around Halloween, kids dress up and go trick-or-treating. Monsters, sports heroes, soldiers, and even some devils roam the streets.

The Bible tells us that we should resist the devil. What do we do with people who dress up like devils? Do we push them away? These verses are not talking about other people, or about putting on costumes. James wants each of us to take a good look at ourselves and then do something about the sin in our lives.

So, how do we resist the devil? Give our will to God and come close to Him. The more we do that, the easier it will be to keep our hands from doing wrong and our hearts from being torn between God's way and the world.

Jesus, thank You for giving me a way to resist the devil! Help me to give You my will and trust You with it. Let me stay close to You. Help me keep my hands and my heart clean. Amen.

88

Pipe-Stacker Blessings

*Let's not get tired of doing what is good.
At just the right time we will reap a harvest
of blessing if we don't give up.*

GALATIANS 6:9 NLT

John got a job at a pipe factory. He was asked to move a stack of pipes from one side of the warehouse to the other. John made sure they were stacked well and secured. The boss was impressed.

The next day the boss asked John to move the pipes back to their original location. John smiled, nodded his head, and carefully moved the pipes back.

For two weeks the boss had John moving the stack of pipes between the two spots. John never complained.

What John didn't know was the boss was looking for a new manager. He'd given this same test to many workers before John was hired. John's willingness and careful work helped the boss see John as someone worth hiring as a manager.

When we do what God asks us to do we may feel like we should be doing something more important. God may have a job for you that will only be possible when you don't give up on your current assignment.

Dear God, You want me to do whatever You ask. You need me to do good things that help others, but also bless others. Help me be patient so I can do what You ask, when You ask, and for as long as You ask. Amen.

89

Christian Hero Defined

Be on your guard; stand firm in the faith;
be courageous; be strong. Do everything in love.
1 CORINTHIANS 16:13–14 NIV

We're all impressed by heroes. That's why we like superheroes who save people from dangerous situations. It's why we read books about people who save the day.

God's Word gives us a great description of what we need in a Christian hero. They're able to tell when something is wrong. They stand guard and make sure bad influences are identified and removed. They stand firm in the faith. They know what the Bible says and do everything they can to follow orders. They are courageous. They know the right thing and they do it. They are strong. They are in the right condition to serve, help, and show honor to God.

Finally a Christian hero shows love in everything he or she does. They know truth, but love stops them from revealing truth in a way that is intended to hurt others. They will use truth to gently point others to God.

All of us can be this kind of hero. When we care more about what God wants than what others think we're on our way.

Heavenly Father, You want me to stand firm, show courage, strength, and love. You want me to show a strength that loves is a quality that people need. Help me follow orders, stand firm, and choose love as my best superpower. Amen.

90

Craving God

*Do not love this world nor the things it offers
you, for when you love the world, you do not
have the love of the Father in you. For the world
offers only a craving for physical pleasure,
a craving for everything we see, and pride in our
achievements and possessions. These are not
from the Father, but are from this world.*

1 JOHN 2:15–16 NLT

We have an enemy who wants to trick us into
trading God things for fun things: a quiet time
for a video game, time in prayer for a basketball game
with friends, Bible study for time with a new comic
book.

God's Word tells us that we will always be offered
a *"craving for. . .pleasure, for everything we see, and
pride in our achievements and possessions."*

The love of the Father (God's love) is an accepting, patient love that changes you and helps you love others. But we often trade God's love for the world's, which is amusing, but never satisfying, always demanding, and loves only itself.

When we replace a hunger for God with a hunger for things that are only fun, impressive, or ego building, then we've made a very bad trade.

Dear God, Your definition of love is so different from what most people accept as love. You warn me not to trade Your gifts for things that are only amusing. They may be fun, but they never satisfy my need to know You. Help me accept Your love and pass it on. Amen.

About the Authors

Glenn A. Hascall is an accomplished writer with credits in nearly one hundred books, including titles from Thomas Nelson, Bethany House, and Regal. His articles have appeared in numerous publications including the *Wall Street Journal*. He's also an award-winning broadcaster, lending his voice to national radio and television networks.

Devotions by Glenn—1, 2, 4, 5, 6, 8, 9, 11, 12, 13, 15, 16, 18, 19, 20, 22, 23, 25, 26, 27, 29, 30, 32, 33, 34, 36, 37, 39, 40, 41, 43, 44, 46, 47, 48, 50, 51, 53, 54, 55, 57, 58, 60, 61, 62, 64, 65, 67, 68, 69, 71, 72, 74, 75, 76, 78, 79, 81, 82, 83, 85, 86, 88, 89, 90.

Tim Baker is the director of student ministries at Trinity Episcopal Church and a professor of biblical studies at LeTourneau University. He's also the editor for *YouthWorker Journal*, a bimonthly publication for adults who work with students. Tim lives in Longview, Texas, with his wife and their three kids.

Devotions by Tim—3, 7, 10, 14, 17, 21, 24, 28, 31, 35, 38, 42, 45, 49, 52, 56, 59, 63, 66, 70, 73, 77, 80, 84, 87.

Calling All Boys! It's time to grow. . .

It All Matters to Jesus Devotional for Boys

Ever wonder if Jesus really cares about your new bike, your favorite app, or how you treat your little sister? Each of the 40 brief devotional chapters in *It All Matters to Jesus* offers reassurance that He does care whether or not you told a "little white lie" at school. . . how you treat Mom and Dad. . .how you spend your free time. . .your daily struggles and cares. . . He cares about every little—and BIG! —thing. Find the heavenly Father in life's daily details and come to know just how much He cares for you!

Paperback / 978-1-63058-921-9 / $5.99

The Comic Book Bible

The Comic Book Bible has educated and entertained tens of thousands of young readers over the past decade and a half! This colorful book for 8–12-year-olds highlights stories from the entire Bible—Genesis through Revelation—with fun artwork and easy-to-understand Bible text.

Paperback / 978-1-60260-685-2 /˙$5.99